Timmy's Time Tale

Written by: Dr. Ngozi M. Obi

Illustrated by: FX and color studio

AuthorHouse™
1663 Liberty Drive
Bloomington, IN 47403
www.authorhouse.com
Phone: 1 (833) 262-8899

Interior Image Credit: FX and color studios

This book is printed on acid-free paper.

ISBN: 978-1-7283-7265-5 (sc)
ISBN: 978-1-7283-7266-2 (hc)
ISBN: 978-1-7283-7264-8 (e)

Library of Congress Control Number: 2020916754

Print information available on the last page.

Published by AuthorHouse 09/18/2020

authorHOUSE®

Dedication

Dedicated to inquisitive children all over the world, may
you never lose your imagination and sense of wonder.

Timmy was excited to get back to Grandma Sarah's house for Sunday Dinner.

It had been awhile.

The car was barely parked in the driveway before he unbuckled his seatbelt and flew out of it.

He didn't bother to wait for his mom and sister.

Timmy ran into Grandma Sarah's arms as she opened the door and stepped outside.

"I've missed you so much!" Timmy exclaimed.

"I've missed you too, Timmy," Grandma Sarah replied.

Timmy hugged her tight.

"Come inside and have a glass of lemonade while we wait for dinner to get ready."

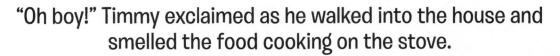

"Oh boy!" Timmy exclaimed as he walked into the house and smelled the food cooking on the stove.

"Everything smells so good, grandma. I can't wait to eat."

"I'm glad because I made all your favorites."

He grinned excitedly at his mom and sister who had finally caught up with him.

"Are Annie and Sam coming too, grandma?"

"Of course, they'll be here."

"Oh boy! When grandma? I haven't seen them in forever."

"Be patient Timmy," Grandma Sarah replied
as she handed him the glass of lemonade.

Timmy tried to be patient but he couldn't wait to see his cousins and play like they used to.

He made his way into the kitchen where Grandma Sarah was finishing making Sunday dinner.

"When will Annie and Sam be here, grandma?"

"Soon Timmy," Grandma Sarah replied.

"How soon is soon, grandma?"

"In about 30 minutes, Timmy."

"What time will that be, grandma?"

"What time is it now?"

"I don't know, grandma. Your clock doesn't have numbers."

Grandma Sarah laughed.

"Guess I'll have to teach you to read time the old- fashioned way with an analog clock."

"What's an analog clock, grandma?"

"One that doesn't only show numbers."

"Ok," Timmy replied.

Grandma Sarah sat Timmy on the counter and started explaining how to read the clock to him.

"You See Timmy, there are 3 hands on the clock."

Timmy nodded to indicate he understood.

"The long hand is the minute hand, the short hand is the hour hand and the tiny one is the second hand," Grandma Sarah continued.

"Ok, grandma."

"There are 12 big lines and 4 small lines after each big line. The big lines are the hours in a day and the small lines are the minutes."

Timmy nodded in agreement.

"You count the hours starting with 12 at the top, then 1, 2, 3 and so on down the right side all the way around the clock until you get back to 12."

Timmy nodded again.

"Every time the tiny hand moves, is 1 second and when it moves all the way around the clock, the minute hand moves once and that is 1 minute."

"Ok, grandma."

"When the minute hand moves all the way around the clock, the hour hand moves once to the next big line and that is 1 hour."

Timmy looked at the clock.

"You read the time as the big line the hour hand is on and the line the minute hand is on."

"Ok, grandma."

"So Timmy, can you tell me what time it is?"

Grandma Sarah asked.

Timmy looked hard at the clock on the wall and tried to put together an answer from all Grandma Sarah just explained to him.

"6 hours 2 minutes," he replied.

"Not quite."

"But grandma the hour hand is on big hour line six and the minute hand is on big hour line two so it's 6 hours 2 minutes."

"Actually its 6:10," Grandma Sarah laughed.

"But why? The minute hand isn't on big hour line ten."

"Let me explain it a little better. Remember I told you the 12 big lines are the hours in a day."

"Yes, grandma. So, there are only 12 hours in a day?" Timmy asked.

"There are actually 24 hours in a day," Grandma Sarah explained.

"Why are there only 12 big hour lines on the clock if there are 24 hours in a day?"

"Because the day is divided into morning and evening."

"It's light outside in the morning and dark outside in the evening," Timmy added.

"Yes, Timmy. When the hour hand goes all the way around the clock the first time, those are the morning hours and it's called AM."

"Ok."

"When it goes around the second time, it's the evening hours and it's called PM."

"Since it's evening now, it's 6hours 2 minutes pm," Timmy Blurted out.

"Not quite."

"Oh brother."

"Each small line after each big hour line is one minute."

"That means the 4 lines after each big hour line are 4 minutes, grandma."

"Actually, from one big hour line to the next big hour line is 5 minutes."

"Why, when there are only 4 small lines between each big hour line?" Timmy asked.

"Because you count from the first small line after a big hour line to the next big hour line which is 5."

Timmy counted it out with his fingers. "You're right, grandma."

"Counting by 5 from big hour line 12 at the top as you go around the clock, each big hour line becomes 0, 5, 10, 15 and so on when the minute hand is on a big hour line," Grandma Sarah pointed out.

"That's like multiplying by 5, grandma."

"Very good. Can you tell me what the time is now based on that?"

"6 hours 10 minutes pm."

"Very close, but you don't have to say hours and minutes. Just say 6:10pm."

"6:12 pm now grandma, the minute hand moved two times already."

"You're so smart, Timmy!"

Timmy grinned.

"If the minute hand is on the big 12 hour line, you only have to say the hour because it's zero minutes," Grandma Sarah added.

"Ok. Grandma, there are 5 minutes from one hour line to the next one, so the minute hand has to move 60 times before the hour hand moves once."

"Yes, Timmy."

"That means there are 60 minutes in 1 hour."

"Absolutely right and the second hand has to move 60 times around the whole clock before the minute hand moves once."

"There are 60 seconds in 1 minute too, grandma."

"Yes, Timmy."

"Wow, grandma."

Timmy jumped off the counter with Grandma Sarah's help and ran into the family room excitedly explaining all he'd just learned to his mom.

"That's awesome, Timmy. Did you tell Grandma Sarah thanks for teaching you to read the clock?"

"Thank you, grandma."

"You're so welcome, Timmy."

"Grandma, the clock in here is easier to read
because it has numbers and big lines."

"Yes, and some have all numbers instead of big lines."

"I can't wait to tell Annie and Sam how to read the clock."

"You'll have plenty of time to do that after dinner," Timmy's mom replied.

"I think I hear them now," Grandma Sarah announced.

Timmy went to the door with her.

He hugged his cousins and started telling them how Grandma Sarah taught him to read time on the wall clock.

Grandma Sarah hated to interrupt the excitement in her living room but they had to get washed up for dinner.

Annie and Sam's mom took all of the kids to the bathroom to wash their hands while Timmy's mom helped Grandma Sarah set the table and put the food on it.

Grandma Sarah insisted they all sit at the dining table together.

The adults helped the kids onto the dining chairs.

Grandma Sarah was pleased. She was happy to have both of her daughters and all of her grandchildren at her table for Sunday Dinner again.

She smiled as she shared the grace.

Activity pages

What time is it?

_____

_____

_____

_____

What time is it?

_____   _____

Draw your own clock

Color your clock

Answer key

6:10

10:00

7:20

12:00

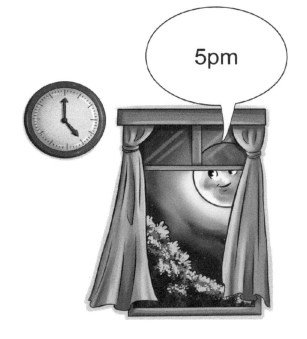